$7.00

WITHDRAWN

PLAINFIELD PUBLIC LIBRARY
126 South Main Street
P.O. Box 305
Plainfield, WI 54966-0305

This story is an illustrated narrative about two young children watching the drilling of a home's water well and the installation of a water pump. In dialog with the well drillers, the children develop an understanding of the process and equipment used to make the well and how water is brought from the ground to the house. A glossary at the end of the story adds explanation of water well drilling specific words.

Watercolor paints and a black pen were used for the full-color art.

Copyright © 2007 by American Ground Water Trust
All rights reserved. No part of this book may be reproduced or utilized in any form or by any means, electronic or mechanical, including photocopying, recording, or by any information storage and retrieval system, without permission in writing from the Publisher, American Ground Water Trust, 16 Centre Street, Concord, New Hampshire, 03301, www.agwt.org.

Printed by Eau Claire Press Company

ISBN (10): 0-9641186-3-7
ISBN (13): 978-0-9641186-3-8

The American Ground Water Trust is a not-for-profit 501(c)(3) education organization incorporated in 1986. Trust education programs throughout the United States focus on:
- Promoting efficient and effective ground water management
- Communicating the environmental and economic value of ground water
- Showcasing ground water science and technology solutions
- Increasing citizen, community and decision-maker awareness
- Facilitating stakeholder participation in water resource decisions

Well...
What's All That Drilling About ?

Written by
Andrew Stone and Jessica Bryan
American Ground Water Trust

Illustrated by
Rachel Pender

My name is Jason and I have a sister named Julie. We live in the country. Our house is next to my dad's workshop. Nearly every day my dad is out in his truck working to make sure that the people who live nearby have water for their homes. Most of them get their water from water wells. My dad is a well driller. His job is drilling deep down underground to reach water in the rocks.

It was very early when the phone rang. I knew it was early because it was still dark outside. I heard my dad say, "Okay, Mr. Hutchins, don't worry. I'll be over in a short while."

A few minutes later I saw the flash of the headlights and heard the growly engine of my dad's truck as it went down our driveway.

"Where did Dad go?" I asked Mom at breakfast.

"There was a storm last night and lightning hit Mr. Hutchins' barn. The pump for his dairy cows stopped working and Dad has gone to fix it," she said.

"When will he be back?" I asked. "He said he would take us with him today."

"Oh, don't worry, he will be back in time to take you and Julie with him," said Mom.

We have been out with Dad before, but today we will see Dad and his crew drilling a new water well from start to finish including putting in the water pump. Dad and his helpers, George and Cindy, make wells to bring water to hundreds of the homes and farms around where we live.

I heard Dad's truck come back. "Hey, Dad, did the cows get their water?" I asked as he came into the kitchen.

"Yes, it was easy to fix the problem. I had to mend a wire that lightning had hit. When I left, the cows had water and Mr. Hutchins was busy with the morning milking."

My school is closed today because of a teachers' meeting. My mom is going to visit my grandpa so my sister Julie and I are going to spend the day with my dad. We won't be allowed to get too close to the drill rig but Dad told us we can watch from the back of his truck.

"Hurry up Julie and Jason," Dad said, "George and Cindy took the drill rig over yesterday so we can get an early start." "If we hurry, we will be there at the very start of the new well. Drillers call it spudding the well."

"Race you to the truck, Jason!" shouted Julie.

"Don't squash your sandwiches!" Mom shouted as we scrambled into Dad's truck.

We drove to the Johnson's new house where the water well was needed. The drill rig and pump truck were already in the front yard. Dad parked next to Cindy's Jeep. Cindy was wearing a yellow hard-hat; the same color as her hair. George had a white hard-hat on. Dad pointed to two extra hard-hats in the pick-up and then pointed to his head. Julie and I put them on.

"The first job is to raise the drill rig's mast," said Dad, "we have to make sure there are no trees or electric wires nearby."

"Get ready, everyone!" Dad shouted as he put on his hard-hat. Suddenly there was a big puff of black smoke as George started up the loud drill rig engine. We watched the mast rise until it was pointing straight up.

"The mast holds the drill rods so they can twist round and round down into the ground," explained Dad.

Cindy and George were wearing ear protectors because of the loud engine and handed us each a set to wear. They hooked a long pipe on a wire cable and a motor on the drill rig pulled it up straight, next to the mast. On the end of the pipe they fixed the special tool that would make the hole.

Dad explained, "This is called a drill bit, and the long pipe it is fixed to is a drill rod."

We watched as George pulled a lever on the drill rig and the drill rods turned slowly round and we saw dirt begin to pile up as the drill bit went down into the ground. Dad explained that the top layers of the ground were soft but that soon the drill bit would reach hard rock.

George and Cindy stopped the drilling to add another drill rod and then the drilling began again. Every few minutes George used a shovel to remove the muddy sand that was coming up the hole. Dad explained that the drill bit was crushing the rocks into small pieces and that air from the drill was forcing up the pieces of soil and rock from the bottom of the hole.

After a while, Julie said, "The water in this well doesn't seem to be any good. It looks like thick mud. You told me there was water under the ground."

"Be patient, I expect that we will have to drill down much deeper. See that tall tree over there? We will have to go deep into the ground, even further down than that tree is sticking up into the air," Dad said.

"How does the water get to be under the ground?" I asked.

"Every time we have heavy rain, some water flows to streams and lakes, but most soaks into the ground. Some is used by trees and plants, and some gets past the roots and seeps deep down underground," Dad explained.

Dad, George and Cindy were busy with drilling deeper into the ground, so we sat in the back of the pick-up and ate our sandwiches. We watched Dad working next to the drill rig with his welding torch making lots of sparks.

Cindy told us that the flame from the welding torch joins two pieces of steel pipe called well casing. "All drilled water wells have casing to stop the top layers of soil from falling into the hole," she explained. "This well has steel well casing pipe, but sometimes we use strong plastic pipe."

Soon there was a steady spray of clear water and Dad said, "Okay, we can stop drilling now."

We watched Cindy fill up some bottles with the well water.

"Are you thirsty?" Julie asked her.

"No," laughed Cindy, "we have to check that the water is safe to drink. I'm taking these bottles to a laboratory to be tested." On the bottle label she wrote the date, the address of the new home and how many feet down they had drilled.

As Cindy drove off in her Jeep, Dad and George were working on the drill rig pulling up the drilling rods, one by one. At the end of the last one was the drill bit. After they had taken off the drill bit, they lowered the drill rig mast. When Cindy came back, George moved the drill rig so she could bring the pump truck right up to the well.

"What's happening now?" Julie asked Cindy.

"We have to put in a water pump that will bring the water from the well into the house," she answered. Cindy explained that the hole the drill bit had made deep into the ground was now filled with water from cracks and spaces in the rocks. The hoist on the pump truck will lower a water pump to the bottom of the well, and when it is turned on, the pump will make water flow through a long pipe from the well to the house.

   Just then, a car drove into the driveway and a man and woman got out. They had a little, fluffy, white dog with them. Dad introduced us to Mr. and Mrs. Johnson who were going to live in this new house where we had just drilled the well.
   My dad explained to them that the house has a good water well and that there is enough water to also use on their yard and garden. With his measuring tape Dad showed them that the drilled well was 150 feet deep.

"We are moving from the city and have never had a water well before," said Mrs. Johnson.

Cindy told the Johnsons that water from their new well had already been taken for testing to make sure it is safe to drink. George explained that all the houses in this area have their own water wells and because well water comes from deep underground it is usually safe to drink.

"We are now ready to lower the water pump into the well," said my dad.

 A shiny, new, silver-colored water pump, long pipe and an electric cable were lowered down into the well by the hoist. When the water pump was down below the water, my dad, George and Cindy set to work to join the pump in the well to the house. The water would go to the bathrooms, the kitchen, the laundry room and to outside faucets for the yard and garden.

　　After watching the water pump go into the well, we all went to see where the pipe bringing water from the well would go into the new house. In this home, the pipe went into the basement.

　　"See here," said George, "this water tank stores some of the well water and when you need more, the pump in the well fills it up again. These pipes that are already in the house will take the water to the kitchen, bathrooms and laundry."

"Every time you turn on the tap you will have cool, fresh water from deep underground," Dad told the Johnsons. "The well water needs to be tested each year to be sure it is still safe to drink." He gave them a notebook that had a lot of information and pictures about water wells, ground water and well pumps.

"Tomorrow your home will have water in every faucet," he said.

"Wonderful!" exclaimed Mr. Johnson. "We couldn't live in a house without water."

Cindy was outside clearing away the mud and rock pieces from around the well. She then used a wrench to fit a cover she called a well cap on the top of the well casing. The red well cap had Dad's name and phone number on it.

"The well cap will stop any dirt or insects from getting into the well," she explained.

It was getting dark by the time we left the Johnson's new house and I was hungry. Julie and I had finished our sandwiches hours ago.

"It's been a busy day," Dad said. "Since Mom will be getting home late from visiting Grandpa, we're going to eat at Bob's Diner."

I had a cheeseburger, Julie had chicken nuggets and my dad had a steak. We all had ice-cream sundaes for dessert.

"I need a good night's sleep. Let's hope there won't be another early morning phone call," said Dad, as we drove into our driveway.

By then it was dark, but as we drove in, I could see the drill rig and the pump truck parked by the workshop, ready to bring water to another home tomorrow.

As I lay in bed I realized I had learned a lot today. I learned that ground water comes from deep underground and there are millions of homes, like the Johnson's, that have their own water wells. How could we live without water for drinking, cooking, washing dishes and laundry or for watering the garden? I think that drilling wells is a very important job.

As I fell asleep, I thought about all the things a well driller needs to know:

He has to work with machines and engines.

He has to know about soil and rocks.

He has to work with electricity and well pumps.

He has to know about water tanks and pipes in the home.

He must know about testing water to make sure it is safe.

And he might have to help fix a water pump at any time of the day or night because families and farm animals have to have water to drink every day. If there is one thing that we all must have, it is water.

I think when I grow up I will be a well driller just like my dad . . .

Glossary

cracks and spaces: Places where water can fit in underground rocks.

drill bit: Very hard metal tool that can grind up rock.

drill rods: Metal rods that are joined together as the well gets deeper.

drill rig: Machine that uses drill rods and a drill bit to make water wells.

ear protectors: Covers to protect a worker's ears from the loud noises of machinery.

electric cable: Thick electric wire that sends electricity to the water pump.

faucet: An on and off tap that lets water flow into a sink, bath or hose.

flows to streams: Water from rain that goes to streams and rivers.

ground water: Water found in cracks and tiny spaces in sand and rocks.

hard rock: Solid rocks such as granite, sandstone or limestone.

hard-hat: Safety hat worn by workers.

hoist: A mast on the back of a truck with a strong wire used to lift or lower heavy pumps and pipes.

laboratory: The place where water is tested to make sure it is safe to drink.

lever: A handle that starts and stops a machine or motor.

mast: The tall upright part of the drill rig that holds the drill rods.

pump truck: A truck that can lower the water pump, pipes and cable into the well.

seeps deep down underground: Water that soaks down and fills up cracks and spaces in the rocks.

soaks into the ground: Rain that goes into the soil. Some will be used by plants.

spudding: Special word used for the very start of drilling a well.

top layers: Top layers of the ground are usually soft soils. Beneath are rocks.

water pump: An electric well pump pushes water from the well to the house.

water well: A drilled hole with casing, pipes and a water pump.

water tank: A place where water from the well is stored.

welding torch: Very hot flame used to melt metal and join two pieces of pipe together.

well casing pipe: Steel or plastic used in a water well to keep out soil or dirty water.

well cap: The special lid used to keep the well and the pump protected.

well driller: Person who uses a drill rig to make water wells.

wrench: Tool used to make a tight fit by turning a metal nut on a bolt.

For more information about

ground water and water wells:

www.privatewell.com

PLAINFIELD PUBLIC LIBRARY
126 South Main Street
P.O. Box 305
Plainfield, WI 54966-0305